Thinking of Basho, Kiyosumi Garden, Sumida District, Tokyo, Japan 1996
(from this garden Matsuo Basho began his lifelong journey *On the Narrow Road to the Deep North*).
© Thomas Joshua Cooper.

Atoms of Delight

an anthology of Scottish haiku and short poems

Atoms of Delight

Edited by Alec Finlay
With a Foreword by
Kenneth White

pocketbooks
Morning Star Publications
Polygon

2000

Published by:
pocketbooks
Canongate Venture (5), New Street, Edinburgh EH8 8BH.

Morning Star Publications
Canongate Venture (5), New Street, Edinburgh EH8 8BH.

Polygon
22 George Square, Edinburgh EH8 9LF.

Typeset in Minion and Univers.
Designed by Lucy Richards and Matthew Chapman, with Alec Finlay.
Printed and bound by Redwood Books Limited, Trowbridge.

Printed on Munken Elk 90gsm available from Trebruk UK Limited.

Published with the assistance of a grant from the Scottish Arts Council National
Lottery Fund and a grant from Highlands & Islands Enterprise (HI Arts).

THE SCOTTISH ARTS COUNCIL
National Lottery Fund

Highlands & Islands
OF SCOTLAND

A CIP record is available from the British Library.

ISBN 0 7486 6275 8

List of Contents

Dedicated to the memory of Iain Crichton Smith 1928-1998.

Guid gear gangs in small bulk

Editor's Acknowledgements

I would like to thank the contributors for their forbearance in what has been a lengthy project. Somewhere close to 10,000 contributions were received, so the work of collating, selecting, and ordering the anthology has been considerable. I would also like to thank: Cluny Sheeler, who worked with me from the project's inception; Ken Cockburn, for his editorial suggestions and calm perseverance; pocketbooks administrator Alison Humphry; Alison Bowden, Ian Davidson and Jeanie Scott at Polygon, and Andrew MacDougall at Scottish Book Source; Lucy Richards and Matthew Chapman for the elegant simplicity of the book's design; Callum Innes and Thomas Joshua Cooper for kindly allowing us to use their work on the front cover and frontispiece respectively; Ian Stephen for reading through the manuscript, not once but three times; Thomas A. Clark for his encouragement; Kevin MacNeil for his help, in particular with the Gaelic contributions. Kevin is now working as the first Iain Crichton Smith Writing Fellow for the Highlands, and it is fitting that this book is dedicated to Iain's memory. I like to think that its contents would have made him smile. The Scottish Poetry Library, National Library of Scotland, City of Edinburgh Library, and University of Edinburgh Library have provided new finds and necessary bibliographic information.

I would also like to thank David Connearn ('Basho'), Tom McGrath, J. B. Pick, Rory Watson, Harry Gilonis, Gerry Loose, Kenneth White, Alan Spence, and my father; their suggestions helped me to shape the original concept. Finally, I would like to make a more personal bow of thanks to Zoë Irvine for what was shared, and to Thomas Evans ('Sora') for his comradeship.

The Haiku Approach

In everybody's experience, there are days when one's personal opacity (the coagulation of the self, the density of being) *lights up*. Like the sky after a storm. One finds one's self in an immense silence, in an extremely pleasant emptiness. At moments such as these, says an old Japanese poet, 'everything is haiku'. You look at a pebble, the branch of a tree, a gesture in the street, and you have the impression that the entire world, the whole of life, is being revealed to you. The difficult thing is not to overdo it – wax over-poetic, for example. That moment, arisen from emptiness, must be allowed to return to the emptiness, without too much interference on your part.

That is the haiku way.

* * *

It was a country hostelry, at dawn, on Honshu island, in the region of Okayama. Somebody had got up even earlier than me. On the frosted window, with one finger, he or she had drawn a mountain: Mt Fuji, of course. That was a haiku moment. The poem (but is it a poem?) came into my head exactly the way the drawing had come to the hand:

Ah! Mount Fuji
drawn with one finger
on a frosted window

That was another life . . .

This morning on the North coast of Brittany, I'm listening to a piece of shakuhachi music (shakuhachi, the flute used by the wandering monks): 'Empty sky'.

I'm thinking of that 'emptiness'.

Of what is the sky 'empty'? Of metaphysical concepts, no doubt, and of sacredness. But not of reality. These last few days, wild geese have been flying over, greylags and whitefronts, on their way from Greenland to Africa.

I'm thinking back to that old haiku. The person (body-mind) that had got up before me had a sense of the sacred: it was Mt Fuji he or she drew. I too recognised it. But neither of us was over-attached to it. We both knew that in a very little time, the sun would be rising and would melt the frost. The sacred symbol would disappear, all you'd have would be a clear window, and beyond it, outside there, the world, phenomenally present.

I push my thought to its limits, I follow my thinking into the emptiness . . .

After the sacred, there was science. In science, you can ask yourself mathematically interesting questions such as this: what's the length of the Breton coast? If you're going to be scrupulous about it, going from cape to cape, from stone to stone, you realise there's no definitive answer.

Once you arrive at that realisation: beyond faith, beyond questioning, you're ready for the haiku road.

* * *

This morning, in the mail, came a poetic almanac from Japan. Inspired by the calendars of Northern China, which take their inspiration from the *I Ching* or *Book of Changes*, these almanacs describe the changing of the seasons, underline the deep links between the stars, spirits, animals, plants and human beings, and, incidentally, provide the 'season words' necessary for the traditional practice of haiku.

You will hear, for example, of *shunsa*, which refers to the festival marking the beginning of the year's work in the fields, or again of *hi gan*, which is the equinox of Spring and Autumn. Haiku, then, is intimately connected to a sensation of time, of weather and the rhythm of the year. On that basis, from there on (I see no need today to be systematically orthodox), it's a question of observation, contemplation, and sometimes, discreetly, erudition. The idea is to grasp a moment in such a way that it opens out onto the whole field of culture, the entire space of the cosmos.

* * *

I've just been reading Jean Giono's book, *Manosque-les-Plateaux*. 'The river Largue', he writes, 'is a series of holes. From these shadowy holes emerge indolent gleaming fish. I used to know their names, but I've forgotten the names on purpose because they got in the way of my vision. Knowing their names won't help me to see the blue spot one has on its head, or the big round teeth another has in its gub, naming won't get me emotionally in touch with their exact and lascivious movements . . .'

That's very close to a phrase by Nansen (783-834), which itself is an echo of Lao-tzu: 'In the age of emptiness, there were no names.' We may remember too Sampu's haiku: 'The names unknown / but every weed has its flower / and its beauty' ('*na wa shirazu / kusa-gota ni hana / aware nari*').

What I mean by these examples is that the essential experience is as much Western as Eastern. Or rather, that it's neither Eastern nor Western. It comes from the Void.

Down to Earth but Close to Heaven

As I write it is the cusp of Easter; snow is falling through the sunshine, falling over the white blossoms of the wild gean outside my window. Slowly the dark earth is turning white. There is a moment when by a trick of the eye it seems as if the blossoms are rising upwards, falling towards the sky. It is a haiku moment.

* * *

A few years ago I found two books of haiku on my father's book shelves. What first drew me to them was their look and their feel. Both were bound in traditional Japanese papers, with hand stitched binding and covers that were delicate but coarse to the touch, as if made from a mixture of rice paper and raffia. Their beauty was in their simplicity; there was no extravagance, no extraneous detail, and they allowed the poems space to breathe. The titles intrigued me: *Cool Gong, Cool Melon*. Printed in Kyoto and containing haiku translated by the American poet Cid Corman, the books perfectly exemplified the vision of life the poetry described. It added a touch of charm that some of the translations had been revised after printing, a blue biro paring away:

> honk of snot
> ~~being~~ blown in the hand
> plum-blossom ~~climactic~~ supreme

Gathering the poems for this anthology has been proof that my affection for haiku is widely shared. At one time I planned to make an anthology containing solely haiku; instead, I have gathered together a number of forms of short poem. These poetic measures – like so many different sized pebbles, each one different in its weight and texture – belong together.

Alongside the Japanese forms of haiku, senryu and tanka, are traditional European forms, such as the couplet, examples of short epigrams and epitaphs, and a few folk cousins in the shape of proverbs. I have also included one line poems (a nineteenth-century invention primarily memorable for its adoption by the French Surrealist poets), monostichs, more recent innovations, such as Concrete haiku, and contemporary forms which are closely associated with one particular poet: Ian Hamilton Finlay and the one-word poem, Thomas A. Clark and dicotyledons, and Gael Turnbull and spaces.

The twentieth century is the second great era of the short poem. The first, the 'grave poems' of the Ancients, most famously the epigraphs and epigrams of Ancient Greece and Rome – also those of the Gaels and Vikings – has been a constant in European poetry since the Renaissance. This tradition is represented here by epigrams and epigraphs by Drummond of Hawthornden, Burns, Scott, Soutar and MacDiarmid, and latterday pastiches such as Alexander Scott's witty 'Scotched' series. W. S. Graham's Heraclitean fragments, 'Implements in Their Places' were much in my mind here, but they are so much part of a sequence I decided not to include excerpts.

This is the largest survey of Scottish haiku and senryu. It traces a love affair between Occident and Orient, from the translations of Oriental poetry that were a crucial influence on Modernism, through the post-war era, when spiritual visions of the East came to pervade popular culture – a century's journey from *Cathay* to *The Dharma Bums* to *Love & Zen in the Hebrides*.

This current of Oriental influence passes through early visitors to Japan, such as Ernest Fennelosa and Lafcadio Hearn, through the lightning conductor Pound, to W. B. Yeats, T. E. Hulme, Arthur Waley and Arthur Cooper; and the Americans Alan Watts, Phillip Lamantia, Lucien

Stryk, Jack Kerouac, Gary Snyder, Joanne Kyger and Allen Ginsberg. It is not exclusive to poets and includes fellow travellers such as D. T. Suzuki, Thomas Merton, John Cage and Brice Marden, and in Scotland artists such as William Johnstone, Alan Johnstone, and Donald Urquhart.

At different times in this century, and in many countries around the World, interest in haiku has amounted to a craze. For instance, following its arrival in Mexico in the early years of the century, poets such as Pacheco, Tablada, and later Octavio Paz, were inspired to publish collections of haiku. In Europe poets as varied as Rilke, Eluard, Machado, Transtömer and Seferis have taken up the form. The haiku tradition has sustained itself as a worldwide phenomenon through its combination of a discrete identity and adaptability. The Western haiku emerges out of this process of translation and adaptation, and has continued to evolve to the extent that it is now possible to consider it as a form in its own right.

What constitutes a Western haiku? Is it the familiar syllable count, 5-7-5; the season-word; the observance of a three line form; the cutting word; the use of a rhyme scheme; a strict adherence to a theme drawn from nature; a Buddhist view of the world; a visual arrangement of words? All of these elements have at different times been considered essential to the form.

The first recognisable haiku in English was written by Ezra Pound in 1913:

In a Station of the Metro
The apparition   of these faces   in the crowd :
Petals   on a wet, black bough.

A year later the Italian poet Giuseppe Ungaretti (1888-1970) wrote this minimalist gem, scribbled down while he was sheltering in the trenches:

M'illumine
D'immensare

In France another soldier poet, Julien Vocance, wrote a book of haiku *Cent Visions du Guerre, One hundred Visions of War* (1915). A more important literary achievement was that of the poet and diplomat Paul Claudel (1868-1955), who was French ambassador to both China and Japan. Claudel's *A Hundred Movements For a Fan* (1926) was in his own words: 'an attempt to apply the principles of Japanese poetry . . . Each poem is very short, only a phrase, enough, just, to support a breath – of sound, feeling, words – or the beating of the wing of a fan'. Claudel highlights the calligraphic aspect of Oriental poetry (parallelling Apollinaire's visual *Calligrames*).

In the Orient writing and painting share the same instrument and are bodied forth in similar gestures. Claudel believed he could find an equivalent in his own language:

Fan   Poems
                                            wr
                              itten on the
                              br
                                            eath

Similar experiments were already taking place in Mexico, such as those of Efrén Rebolledo and José Juan Tablada, published in the 1920s and '30s. Their work is part of the Hispano-American avant-garde which included the Chilean poet Vicente Huidobro (1893-1948) and the Noigandres Concrete poets of Brazil who came to the fore in the 1950s, and whose influences included Webern, Pound and haiku. This movement parallels many of the later developments in Scotland, where a similar mixture of folk and high art aesthetics were at work. Edwin Morgan translated some of these minimal Brazilian Concrete poems, and they inspired his 'Summer Haiku' (1960), in which these influences coalesce:

Summer Haiku

P o o l .
P e o p l
  e   p l o p !
C o o l .

   Scotland came late to this engagement with Modernism and haiku-influenced forms. MacDiarmid's achievement closely parallels Pound's, moving from the short Oriental or Imagist influenced lyric towards the epic; however, a distinctive tradition of experiment only emerged in the wake of the Beat and Concrete Poetry movements when these traditional and avant garde influences combined in a post-modern melange of playful experiment. A path leads from Morgan's translations of the Noigandres poets, Ian Hamilton Finlay dedicating his first haiku inspired book to the Japanese poet Shimpei Kusano, William Johnstone's calligraphic brush drawings of the early 1970s, to Samye Ling, the Tibetan monastery which nestles in the Border hills, close by Johnstone's hill farm, and later Alan Spence's *Glasgow Zen*.

   The origins of this Scottish-Oriental path lie in Neil Gunn's chance discovery of Zen in 1955 – although Gunn's interest in the East begins at least as early as *Highland River* (1937), in which Hindu Yoga is used as a comparison for Kenn's transcendent journey up the Strath to the river's source. Gunn turned towards the East in his final book, the semi-autobiographical memoir *The Atom of Delight* (1956). Rather than mediating this journey into the Highland landscape of his childhood through the familiar narrative of his novels, here he leads us 'behind the eyes' into a 'mental scenery', guided by Eugen Herrigel's classic study *Zen in the Art of Archery*.

   In other writings from this late period Gunn extends this connection between Zen and his experience of the Highland landscape. The uncanny sense of otherness which the wilderness provokes in him is released from the temporal continuum of the 'Western eye'. Crucial to this enquiry is 'Highland Space' (1961), an essay discussing the paintings of the sixteenth-century Zen master Sesshu, in which Gunn confronts: ' . . . the "vacant" places, brooding mountains, sterile distances . . . the appalling outward swoop into space itself, into infinite emptiness . . . So fundamental does this seem that one takes it as a permanent, if submerged, element in our mental make-up.'

The vertiginous experience of Gunn's solitary wanderer dwarfed against the jagged skyline and the infinite void beyond, diverges from MacDiarmid and Sorley Maclean's epic long poems set against the mountains of Scotland. Their work remains within the European tradition of the sublime whereas what stands out in Gunn's essays is a sense of release from the weight of Highland history. Where his more famous novels charted the psychological dislocation and cultural devastation imposed by the Clearances an imaginative shift occurs in his later autobiographical and contemplative work. Herringel and Sesshu inspired Gunn to reaffirm the Highland epiphany at the centre of his work, and although he would write no more novels, in these late essays he restated his metaphysical perspective and his longstanding dissatisfaction with the proscriptive arguments of 'MacDiarmidism'.

Many of the young Scottish Beat poets shared Gunn's desire to escape the narrow political and cultural horizons the Scottish Renaissance seemed to present. The short poem now emerged as a corrective balance to the MacDiarmidian epic. The first Japanese inspired experiments were Ian Hamilton Finlay's *Glasgow Beasts* (1960), closely followed by Edwin Morgan's translations of haiku influenced Brazilian Concrete poems. For all their inventiveness Finlay and Morgan did not pursue a personal identification with Oriental culture. However, for the generation that followed formal experiments tended to be of less importance than the increasingly popular spirituality of the East made famous by Kerouac, Ginsberg and the Maharishi.

The first Scottish haiku were written by Tom McGrath, sometime in the mid 1960s. A number of poets of his generation turned to the form, for instance, Alan Spence (who published the first collection of haiku by a Scottish poet, *plop!*, in 1970), Alan Jackson, Thomas A. Clark and Kenneth White. Since then parallels between the East and the Highland landscape, and aspects of Scottish (or specifically Gaelic) culture and identity have been replayed with many variations. It is a peculiar leitmotif, this overlaying of the Shirakawa barrier and Isle of Sado over the Cullins and the Hebrides, evidence of a stepping-stone in the process of cultural evolution beyond MacDiarmidite literary nationalism, towards the more plural vision of Scottish culture that emerged in the post 1979 referendum period.

Thomas A. Clark and Kenneth White, have explored these analogies in some depth. White in terms of sacred visions in ancient Shinto and Celtic cultures, and the parallels between Zen and Celtic Christianity, the 'gnostic naturalism' he outlines in his essay 'The Birds of Kentigern'. In books such as *The Frog Leaps Thirteen Times*, *The Sayings of Huang Po* and *Pebbles In A Zen Garden*, Clark combines the clarity of vision and vivid descriptive powers common to Gaelic nature poetry and haiku. For both poets Scotland and Japan share a hyperborean imagination. They wander through the mountains with a book of haiku in their rucksack, neatly tucked alongside a volume of *Carmina Gadelica*. Artists such as Hamish Fulton, Richard Long and Thomas Joshua Cooper, who have made many walks through the Highlands, have a Zen or haiku-influenced art practice and their work can be seen as another branch of this Scottish-Oriental tradition.

Other Scottish poets have employed Oriental analogies, but in terms of contemporary life rather than sense of place. Iain Crichton Smith's

'Chinese Poem' perfectly illustrates this overlaying of Scottish and specifically Gaelic culture with Oriental culture. A Tang Dynasty alter ego is employed to great effect, mimicking the stylistic traits of Gaelic translations, and, in his the poet's words: '[looking at] Scotland in a slightly comic and critical light . . . from a strange perspective.'

A number of other contemporary poets have wandered along these Scottish-Oriental pathways: Gerry Loose, whose best haiku come close to the austere tenderness of Basho; Alan Spence, who alights on the warm humanity revealed in the mundane, and whose haiku continue the warm observations of city-life Finlay introduced in *Glasgow Beasts*; Andrew Greig, whose long poem *Western Swing*, is a contemporary Scottish-Tibetan Beat epic; Frank Kuppner, who strikes a similar vein to 'Chinese Poem' in *A Bad Day for the Sung Dynasty* (1983); Ron Butlin, whose collection of imitations of Ancient Chinese poetry *The Exquisite Instrument* (1982), contains some of his finest love poems, and most recently Kevin MacNeil, whose 'Loo-is Hai-koo' make amusing use of the native vernacular. These poets couldn't be further away from MacDiarmid's idea of a nation of Gaelic speakers living the 'true racial life'.

The great weakness of this cultural voyaging – or tourism – has always been its tendency to sentimental exoticism. However, these Scottish writers use the Orient as an almost transparent veil, through which they peek at and occasionally tease their native land. Their concern is with life in contemporary Scotland now – with 'the swish of Mrs Macleod's pants drying on the line' – and more often than not this saves them from Orientalism. Their work is a cultural bridge between the Byres Road of the 1960s, populated by wandering beat poets and bearded hippies dreaming of India, and the Byres Road of today, filled with take-aways and corner shops. From the streets of 'Glasgae and Faislabad' a new Scottish literature is emerging, as for instance, in the work of a young Indian-

Scottish doctor from Glasgow, Suhayl Saadi, whose first published poems are included here.

* * *

The editors of Scottish poetry anthologies frequently stake a claim for poets as the hand-maidens of political and cultural self-determination. The fate of the short poem, ignored by most anthologists, is an example of how poetics and politics easily slip out of kilter. Whether through conservatism or the prejudice that the short poem is of necessity slight, editors have routinely excluded them from most modern anthologies. Surely though, the Scottish psyche has always been drawn to the diminutive: we live in a country where the 'wee' is still held in affection.

The popularity of haiku may wax and wane, but over the past decade or so, it has undergone one of its periodic resurgences. In Britain this has been supported by the British Haiku Society (formed in 1990). *Blythe Spirit*, the journal published by BHS, provides a valuable critical forum, while recent anthologies *The Haiku Hundred* and *Anthology of British Haiku* (both published by Iron Press) have met with considerable commercial success.

The shortest traditional poetic forms in Scots and Gaelic literature follow four line verse schemes. As these are predominantly used in longer narrative poems I have felt justified in excluding them from this survey, which is largely focussed on Latin and Oriental short forms and what they have become. In such a heterogeneous gathering I have also felt it valuable to include Appendices with two examples of five line forms: the tanka, a traditional Japanese form related to the haiku, and the cinquain.

Atoms of Delight does make an argument, but it would be wrong to suggest that there is a single conclusion to be drawn from presenting these poetic forms in proximity. They delight through their simplicity and the pure intensity of concision, and through openness, wit and humour. These different forms are not ultimately rhetorical devices, but utterances within which the moment can be apprehended and felt. The poems pivot. The one-word poem and haiku turn in a similar way, suggesting the mind dancing from one perception to another – recalling once again the origins of haiku in the single gesture of hand and brush over ink and paper, or, as Bachelard describes, 'a flicker of the soul'.

* * *

There is a beach on the Hebridean island of Berneray around which the flat sea seems gathered in a great chalice, stretching from Skye and the mainland to the east, Uist to the south and the Long Island of Harris and Lewis to the north. Sitting there in the white sand the waves seem to flow towards and away from one at the same time. Once again, it is a haiku moment, putting me in mind of Basho's haiku describing the Milky Way seen over the isle of Sado:

rough as the sea is
reaching over to Sado
the Heaven's star stream

Version by Cid Corman

Alec Finlay

Bibliography

Japanese Haiku Translations

R. H. Blyth, *Haiku*, Vol.s I-IV, (Hokuseido, 1952)

Basho, *On Love and Barley: Haiku of Basho*, translated by Lucien Stryk, (Penguin Classics, 1985)

Basho, *Oku-no Hosomichi, Back Roads to Far Towns*, translated by Cid Corman, (*Origin* magazine: Second Series, No. 14, July 1964; reprinted by White Pine Press)

Basho, versions by Cid Corman, *Cool Gong, Cool Melon* (Origin: Kyoto 1960)

Shiki, *Peonies Kana: Haiku by Upsaka Shiki*, translated & edited by Harold J. Isaacson, (George Allen & Unwin: London, 1973)

Western Haiku

The Haiku Hundred, ed. Kirkup, Cobb and Mortimer, (Iron Press: North Shields, 1992)

Iron Anthology of British Haiku, ed. Cobb and Lucas, (Iron Press: North Shields, 1998)

William J. Higginson, *The Haiku Handbook*, (Kodansha: New York, 1985)

The Haiku Anthology, ed. Cor Van Den Heuvel, (Simon & Schuster: New York, 1986)

Jack Kerouac, *Poems All Sizes* (City Lights Books: San Francisco, 1992)

Bruce Leeming, *Scots Haiku* (Hub Editions, 1995)

Scottish

Thomas A. Clark, *Tormentil and Bleached Bones*, (Polygon: Edinburgh, 1993)

Thomas A Clark, *Pebbles from a Japanese Garden*, with drawings by Laurie Clark, (Topia Press: New York and Bradford, 1977)

Ian Hamilton Finlay, *The Dancers Inherit the Party and Glasgow Beasts*, edited by Alec Finlay, (Polygon: Edinburgh, 1996)

Neil Gunn, *The Atom of Delight* (Faber & Faber: London, 1956)

Tom McGrath, *Buddha Poems*, n.d.

Kevin MacNeil, *Love & Zen in the Outer Hebrides*, (Canongate: Edinburgh, 1998)

Kenneth White, *The Blue Road*, (Mainstream: Edinburgh, 1990)

Kenneth White, *Travels in the Drifting Dawn*, (Mainstream: Edinburgh, 1989)

Kenneth White, *On Scottish Ground: Selected Essays*, (Polygon: Edinburgh, 1998)

Kenneth White, *L'Anorak du goëland*, (L'Instant Perpetuel, 1985)

Other References

Paul Claudel, *A Hundred Movements For a Fan*, translated by Andrew Harvey & Iain Watson, (Quartet Encounters: London, 1992)

Poor.Old.Tired.Horse: one-word poems issue, edited by Ian Hamilton Finlay, (Wild Hawthorn Press, 1967)

Roy Rogers magazine: one-word and one line poems issue (New York, 1973)

Haiku & Senryu

another day
another dream
dawning

Larry Butler

Morning. The haiku
are writing
themselves.

Tom McGrath

From Yokohama Bay to the Mull of Kintyre

The Sound of Snow
Old Hakuin
listening to the snow
out there at Sinoda

Kenneth White

washing trimmed leeks in
icy water thinking of long
ago japan

Lesley Lendrum

There is snow on the mountains.
I know a Japanese professor
who speaks Gaelic.

Iain Crichton Smith

Invented Haiku
Frog jumps
in the water.
Not a sound.

Tom McGrath

Japanese Haiku Owersett Frae Inglis Translations

Reeshlin thegither –
Heids o barley,
Butterflee.

Lady Kan-Jo

Auld puil.
Lowp-splyter!
A puddock!

Buson

Ower the stanes
Traivels the sang
O the winter burn

Ito

Snaw in the gloamin
Taps at the yett
The soun is saft

Joyo

Daybrak.
The storm beeriet
In the snaw

Shiro

versions by Sheena Blackhall

Three Haiku by Issa

it's rainin,
the wean's in
dancin aboot wi
the kitten

disnae matter
how ye look at it –
ma heid's cauld

jist this,
jist this;
still . . .

Alan Spence
after the English translations of R. H. Blyth

That autumn morning
on the waters of the Sumida
one lone gull

At Shirakawa
no poem, no song
only the rain

In the mountains
on the bank of a torrent
drinking cold sake

Green pine
growing on the heights
century after century

North country:
that bear print
on the post-office wall.

Kenneth White

Calendar

first warmth of spring
I feel as if
I have been asleep

the cat swipes at the breeze,
shadow-boxing with
nothing-I-can-see

summer evening –
through the open window,
an old song

warming my feet
in the patch of sunlight
on the floor

autumn cold
the cat's rough tongue
on the back of my hand

damp leaves drift to earth
the sun hangs tangled
in the branches of a tree

rain falling,
especially
on me

the rain has stopped
the sky is clear
come out and look
at the stars

beginning of winter
in the chill
of the milk-bottles

snow falling
everything
in its place

Alan Spence

Spring

A cold spring evening;
opening the door,
the smell of the sea

John Mayhew Manson

In a tree beside
the crematorium
thrushes nesting

Bruce Leeming

enough the larksong
the waves and rain-blurred mayweed
a step from my door

Lesley Lendrum

Kissing in a field
where peewits lay dappled eggs
with cloud courting cloud.

Tom Pow

the grey and yellow
catkins are gently sampled
by an early bee

Lesley Lendrum

after rain
fine grasses – seen leaning
on the washed air.

Scott Eden

The Lambing
Making their debut,
Together on the green baize
Spot-lighted in the sun.

Joanne MacKay

Summary

Thom Nairn

The sun eases itself down
Like a fat man
Into a cold bath

Larry Butler

in botanic gardens
ice cream eaters and cameras
surround the lotus

Ken Cockburn

Lemons, too high up
to pick – but, scenting my palms
till sleep, a windfall.

Colin Will

A wispy cloud drifts up,
Skimming spruce-tops,
Exhaling, the hills huff.

Furious mother
dressed only in a towel –
giggling from the woods.

John McDonald

country road
too dark to see the flowers
but their scent is yellow

Alan Spence

Tapering clouds, like
Flame-brushes, paint the sunset
On the evening sky.

R. L. Cook

One pink sock, one blue
she dips at the water's edge:
it's the litmus kid!

Billy Watt

Autumn

the door bangs back
on its hinges
and in come the leaves

Alan Spence

sleeping alone again
the first time in years
the sound of rain

Gerry Loose

A few leaves
disturb the stillness.
A few footsteps.

Frank Kuppner

sunburnt cheek
from watching the geese
go west.

Davy Polmadie

Drinking tea
in a woolly hat. Sipping it
as the trees go bare.

Scott Eden

The night sky glitters
like a broken engagement.
Who courts autumn now?

Tom Pow

    rain
not raining
     in squalls

Gerry Loose

Spring
Reeshlin, reeshlin, reeshlin
The lang girse fuspers
Memories o Spring.

Sheena Blackhall

Winter

on her coat
brought indoors
the smell of cold

Gerry Loose

A last dignity
undressing in arctic winds
realising its cold.

John Hudson

Stiff winter grasses
nothing moving but the wind –
old men's bones cracking.

John McDonald

Two small boys
in quilted anoraks
are eating snowballs

Billy Watt

Footprints in the snow
walking away
from the wind.

Hamish Turnbull

saying bless me
alone
with a cold

Lindsay Cooper

Snow lies deep.
Is above all argument.
I pass, and leave my footprints to the moon.

G. F. Dutton

Silent lochside
snowswept: landmarks
disappearing

Bruce Leeming

Moon Viewing

Suddenly awake:
such light –
a full moon

John McDonald

Cold winter evening –
moon over the mountain
my only companion.

Anne Tall

the moon moves with us
as we walk,
drifts from tree to tree

Alan Spence

The moon
above a petrol station
in Argyll.

Iain Crichton Smith
translated by kevin macneil

the night's white eye
ball of milk in deepest-blue
october moon

aonghas macneacail

So familiar, so remote –
her face in death,
the journeying moon.

Anne Tall

A sliver of moon
vicious as a kitten's claw
scratches the twilight.

Valerie Thornton

Across the window –
moon moves one way –
clouds move the other

John McDonald

Birds

Coastal aesthetics
Black, white-black, black-white-red:
a quick flight of oystercatchers
over the grey sea

Kenneth White

stretched out in the grass
eyes closed, gull, redshank, plover
call the distances

Thomas A. Clark

Surpliced in downy
White, haloed with foaming spray
Gulls people the sky.

R. L. Cook

twa scarts jist a fit
abune the skinklan watter
flee intil sundoon

Stewart McGavin

Dawn: in the garden
The wakening birds compile a
Palimpsest of song.

R. L. Cook

        the hovering kite
snaps back
        the wind

Gerry Loose

Failed again
trying to describe
the colour of blackbirds.

Colin Will

Bird-song and a slow
gathering of simple shapes,
just these are enough.

Derek Ross

gannet

with folded wings
a gannet strikes into the still sea
and is reunited with its image of itself

oyster-catcher

oyster-catcher wading at the tide line
will dip her head and break
the semblance of herself in the shining water

heron

heron is an obdurate elongation
ghosting the fluid screens
of his speared vision

Angus Martin

A crow
skimming over the sea-rocks?
the shadow of a gull

On the frost of the garden
the paw-prints of the cat
on his way to the woods

This evening over Gwenved
at the setting of the sun
every gull is a rosy gull

Kenneth White

Burds & Beasts

A burd i the sounless air
unkennin o men's dreams
kennin its ain sang.

Up on the muir
the whaups wheipils. Dounby
the bul rowts.

The hare's een pyk't oot
its paws reid wi tryin
ti birze awa the derk.

A ettil sum day
ti flie til the muin, but nou
A hae the hens ti feed.

David Purves

Graybacks
lowpin slee:
hou quait the sprots

Dreich the day:
the craws cannae fash thirsels
croupin

A whaup's wheiple
lane amang the hills –
bairnheid mindins

Birlin doun
the rowth o gean blume
taigles a bummer

I the mirknin paurk
heilant beasts staun lown:
gaffs frae the change

Bruce Leeming

Cuddies

the horse is the distance
   it gazes into without
      knowing what it gazes into

Colin Donati

The old horse
stands staring
into the wind.

John McDonald

fourteen donkeys
in a field
fourteen donkeys!

Alan Spence

a tethered donkey
a small locality in
the grain of the dusk

Thomas A. Clark

Memories of horses
grass slips downhill
greeting the shoreline

Steve Allan

In the high country
That branch among the fern
was a red stag
sheltering from the rain

Kenneth White

Leithen Water Sunny Slope
By the dry-stane dyke
a scattering of black-faced
ewes, green tup, whin-chats.

Alexander Hutchison

graceful
hanging nowhere
cobwebs

Lindsay Cooper

Ben Vorlich

sunlit water-droplets
cascading from a mossy slab –
a hundred diamond necklaces

Loch Lomond's multi-islets,
seen from this green height,
are micro-continents, in a mini-ocean

Loch Sloy is laned
into dark water strips
by blown foam

Driving through Dumbarton
a cherry blizzard strikes
and everybody's smiling.

i the auld bothie
the smaa oors, an aye beddit
hiss o a primus.

aa day on the skis
abune the mist on Glas Maol
wi bleezan bogles

the rig o Garbh Bheinn
near the tap, hauden
by ma freen abune.

on the wey doun
the taste o
blaeberries

pie an beans
mince an tatties
an morangie.

Stewart McGavin

Limit
Pines dancing
in the icy wind –
north of nothingness

Spring Morning in the Mountains
Young mountain peak
take off that shift of mist
so I can see your snowy nakedness

Village of smoke
hills in white mist
mountain whiteness

Ben Lawers
A lone ptarmigan
on the bare grass of the ridge.
Then loose rock, swift cloud.

Chris Powici

on the hill's edge
cloud forming – on the cloud's edge
feathers in the wind

David Platt

Last night
a fog
this morning
a mountain

Hamish Turnbull

Maisic heich the bens
sangs proggin the grund
a cleuch in atwein.

Neil R. MacCallum

Roses & Thorns

searching, the firefly
illuminates his own path –
and still he is lost

chilly wind – my mind
wrenches from the harshness of
its subtle probing

so gentle, the rose
allows even the rude boy
to know her fragrance

the nightingale
sings so sweetly even
crickets stop to listen

roses and thorns come
up together – I turn
eyes to avoid myself

Thomas Joshua Cooper

Orkney Haiku

Waves wash in, out, in,
menhirs incline to each other:
farmers grumbling.

A lift from a lobster fisherman
with red hands. Driving slowly
up and down farm tracks, life on the sea bed.

Kathleen Jamie

from Ham Voe Haiku

Hamnafield and me
this morning: my pluming breath,
its scribbles of scree.

Among chains and rope,
lashed here all winter: Swallow,
Lively, Brighter Hope.

Mandolin, guitar:
after Hurricane Highlights
a slow island air.

No more shag. A joke.
A minute's silence while my
pipe goes up in smoke.

A burst bale at Ham
makes a spread for two ponies,
a bed for one lamb.

Boat-wreck in the nousts,
millstones in moss by the burn.
Windmill blades turn, turn.

How pleasant the walk
to Da Kame from Hamnafield,
in and out of fog.

Let's sort out these names:
Da Sneug, Da Noup, Hamnafield,
Soberlie, Da Kame.

When he's quite certain
I've been here a week, he moves
in my direction.

Bryan, hour by hour,
stoops to the weld: a tiny
flickering flower.

Alistair Peebles
Foula, 1998

Eddies

only failing sight
puts an end to the stars
in coalbucket night

behind the coulter
a thousand mouths appear
white gulls fleck the dark earth

Meltwater and rain.
By the bridge, ducks wait for food
paddling hard.

Flat sea, flat sky,
seaweed frozen on the storm-beach.
Oystercatchers just stand

nets cast to catch fish
thick as stars in the sky
moon gleams slip through the mesh

ideas are eddies
in the river of words
whorls spinning downstream

The season moves from
dark to light. The dazzle hides
the turning mirror

The moon pours her fulness.
Brimful of fish and water
Earth tips away

the fishing boat ploughs
across the night-black sea
making a perfect furrow

in the kist of stone
the enchanted loom
weaves words and music

Angus Dunn

Windy summer morning –
At the bus-stop,
A woman with a lit cigarette
In either hand.

(Edinburgh)

The tent is packed:
Rainbow on mountains –
And now the wind
Blows milk from my spoon!

(Loch Morlich, Glen More)

Across the steely loch:
The full weight
Of the cloudy sky
Pressing down on Ben Hiant.

(Tobermory to Kilchoan ferry)

The boar-inscribed stone,
The rainwater footprint;
And round this ragged rock
The howling wind.

(Dunadd, near Kilmartin)

Back from Scotland –
At the end of the motorway,
The arch of a rainbow
Through which we know we have passed.

(M1, near Watford)

Ma bha tobar an seo,
tha i tioram.
Tha an cladh ri taobh
a' fàs.

Nuair a chì thu rathad,
bi a' gul
nach eil baile aig a' cheann.

Aird Mhòr, Peigh'nn Albannach,
Glac Gugaraidh,
Torr Bàn – bailtean
fo fhraineach.

As t-samhradh,
feur a' mhonaidh lùbte,
a' ghaoth a' dol troimhe
ag ràdh ssh!

Dh'fhalbh na bàtaichean
a seo a Chanada
mar dh'fhalbhas sgòth.

If there was a well here,
it's dry.
The graveyard beside it
grows.

When you see a road
cry
that there isn't a township at the end.

Ardmore, Penalbanach,
Glac Gugaraidh,
Torr Bàn – villages
under bracken.

In summer,
moorgrass bent,
the wind passing through
saying ssh!

The boats disappeared
from here to Canada
like a cloud.

Myles Campbell

Loo-is Hai-Koo

The lash of a harsh
Loo-is rain. Endless moo-ur
and God's loneleeness.

In the graveyard a
ministur playeeng frisbee
with his eldur son.

on the tshurtsh bell
purtshd sleepeeng
a butturfly.*

kevin macneil
*after Buson

A fisherman in big boots,
his lover
and his mother.

A girl
reading the Bible for seven years
waiting for a sailor.

A croft.
Two brothers.
Potatoes on a plate.

Glasgow
in a world of nylon
and of neon.

Iain Crichton Smith
translated by kevin macneil

Dyke
you've to bend backward
till pressure lifts from the nerve
seeing how stones lie

Ian Stephen

Cnoc na Tùrsa, Calanais
Hill of Mourning, Callanish
that I could be
as a tongue of sunlight
drawing slowly over Harris

kevin macneil

Stars swing over Laxdale
They know their turn'll come again
when upstart comets pass

James Miller

slow dull Aurora
steaming over hot Laxdale
make with the Strathspey

Ian Stephen

Sashimi in Frankfurt,
fugu's toxic tingling
nickel on the tongue

Colin Will

Answers
a lang day tying
multimonofilament
stealthy cups of tea

Jim Inglis

one of ours?
in the fairy loch
a satellite (faint)
winking

kevin macneil

Why did he return
to that empty island?
bog-cotton in the wind

Kenneth White

a blue without flaw
without centre or limit
a deep even blue

coming to the edge
of the forest, a moment
of hesitation

deep moss beneath pines
silence, clarity, fragrance
going on and on

a pool among trees
a place where the stillness can
look back at itself

a small stream tumbling
out of shadow into light
then back to shadow

alder roots, mossy rocks
interruptions in a flow
produce melody

a soft light has found
its way through the foliage
to rest on the trunk

hidden, revealed, veiled
the whole of the mountain
implied behind cloud

sitting on a stone
on the island of the dead
looking at mountains

high inside myself
I watch the rain approaching
from a far country

sorrow like a rock
solid and impervious
dark throughout its mass

a long forest road
so tired of myself I scream
three deer run in gloom

with care, taking care
a curlew wades out into
a dazzling expanse

if walking alone
I am lonely it is both
a place and a path

Reading Erigena
in the Atlantic super-express:
vistas of periphyseonic space

Hearing seamews
but when I raised my head
only the moon

Around this workroom
listen to it prowling
the wind of the earth

This early snow
makes you want to read
only words full of silence

Ah, those Spring days
on the Eastern shores
on the Western shores

Kenneth White

Interiors

A rose in a bowl on the TV set,
the things that are in the world,
the things that are not.

Iain Crichton Smith

smell of my father's house
strange
after only a year

Lindsay Cooper

reflecting
    in the shadowed room
eye of the rockinghorse

Anne McKay

The small jar
has bent
the goldfish.

Hamish Turnbull

window
too high to see
sound of rain

Lindsay Cooper

bereft of time and hope
the scabby old cat looks round
forlorn like a poetry magazine

Francis Gallagher

Dundee Haiku
Shoals of assistants
jink in the fishpond behind
McLeish's counter

Kate Armstrong

Communication
Blue evening light
over Lannion Bay –
I pull out the telephone plug

Kenneth White

City-life

Point of departure
Nothing much in the Rue d'Ecosse
that dark little cul-de-sac –
just the full moon and a stray cat

Kenneth White

something has gone wrong –
the workmen stand and stare
in the cold rain

Alan Spence

stormy morning
the tenements stand still
the sun zips about

Valerie Gillies

night in the city
lights in towerblocks going out
1 by 1

Sean Burn

wokkin hame
how glammurus
lit up
thi late nite bus

Alison Flett

A perfect circle
of discoloured grass –
torn posters

John McDonald

A lark singing
sublimely: our milkman
whistling out of tune

Bruce Leeming

Hitch-Haiku
nae hat
an the cauld rain fallin
    – dearie me

Alan Jackson

Three Senryu

E'en athort the bey
yatt lichts gliff yallochie
– tassies plinkin

Daunerin blithe
i the caul – kiltit callan
trousered lass!

Ladin the deid-kist
intil the pail – ane chiel
lunts a gun

Redundant
pit pony
afraid of the sun.

Off the high board
his body
dives into its shadow.

On parade
a yawn
passing down
the line.

Boats & Voyages

Mainsail
gooseneck and spars
tense to a battened beat
greylag cloth

Ian Stephen

drum drumming
drum drumming your fingers
on the steering wheel
rain on the skerry

kevin macneil

North-West
A grey shore
and a battered herring-box:
Scott of Stornoway

Kenneth White

haaf nets dryin
wi ilka tirl –
anither scale fawin

Colin Maxwell-Charters,
translated into Scots
by Rev. W. G. Pritchard

The tide comes in –
boats rise,
tug at their moorings

John McDonald

Table
elm anticyclones
tight grain in deepening lows
occluded meetings

Ian Stephen

Moon over the Clyde;
the marker buoys wink across
redgreen, redgreen; white . . .

Billy Watt

helm fiddles wavebands
she doesn't need much steering
diesel bodhrans beat

Jim Inglis

Thud, thud, thud –
the boat coming up the river
dead slow under the rain

Kenneth White

tidal tangle tints
from the belly of the bay
every known sailcloth

Ian Stephen

Maeve
on the cliff-edge against a gale force 7
she takes an airbath in a starshape
nothing to hold her back

Valerie Gillies

tide
the exposition of tide:
that under its shifty waters
there is solidity after all

Angus Martin

Last Obsequies
Hands on gunwhale – to the noust
haul this weathered yawl:
there leave her, safely housed.

Robert Rendall

Damaged boats
propped up on the grass –
all facing the sea.

John McDonald

waukrife hauf the nicht
wi thochts o the wee burns
rinnan thir lee lane

Lesley Lendrum

Drifting in a boat,
solitude for company,
trying out new lines.

Richard Burton

Thus' ann a Leòdhas
mise seòladh na mara
'n aon ghealach ar n-acair.

You, in Lewis
while I sail the sea
the one moon our anchor

Angus Macmillan

On Berneray

scurrying legs, wings
a pale cluttered clutch
– MacCaig's sandpiper's

that muddied turquoise
across from stolen mountains
mist, gale together

sealnecks stretch from tan
Harris hills returned to us
– shared references

birch-bark undertow
Berneray luffs, underway
cream flax flying-jib

our own patched main
powers landmass
– island leaves its sound

Ian Stephen

Marram: A Hebridean Renga

sea-bourne boundary
separated from high ground
water moving close

stalks, sharp, whitening
holding sand against the sea
piercing into blue

ripening harvest
marram shelter coiling green
weaves into life

marram bends to pressure
scythed by low declining sun
equinox passes

the noise of stones
tangle, touch it, cold alone
a difference here

(Taigh Chearsabhagh, 1998)
Janice Fraser, Abigail Ingledew,
Margaret Maclellan, Catherine
Muir, Fiona Pearson

Loving

A morning rose
dawn sunlight
– just so, your breasts.

Iain Crichton Smith
translated by kevin macneil

All shells and bones
   the spey-wife enters,
      widdershins.

Kathleen Jamie

we go walking
only one shadow
cast on the wall

Valerie Gillies

You, my love, are dearer to me
than Softly Softly
than Sportsnight with Coleman.

Iain Crichton Smith

endless afternoon
another day
and no letter

Lindsay Cooper

Doun i the haugh
dwammy wi haw flourish
a wumman greitin

Bruce Leeming

home
still, when I round the
corner, your window shining
with no light in it.

Anne Macleod

A.M.
'Dè mun a tha thu?'
Wet, your hair gleams. Heather dew.
Gems. Dharmadhatu.

kevin macneil

dè mun a tha thu? – how are you?
dharmadhatu – the universe as perceived in enlightenment,
often imagined as a myriad of sparkling jewels

Sampled

orbit out your dreams
and with wider wilder turns
you grow more lovely

the sweet south sampled
and sharp tasty hip hop grooves
heavy street night air

stealing and giving
our scents touching and blending
your colours and mine

it is so sweet now
I could never get enough
turn it up play on

Elspeth Murray

Ya mo me, widow,
meaning frost woman: beyond
sensuality.

Mi bo jin, widow,
meaning not yet dead person:
all purpose denied.

Slip from your shadows;
annihilate dominion.
Shake off those grave clothes.

*A haiku series exploring Japanese
meanings of widowhood.*

Christine De Luca

In the cauld blast
Each desperate tree
cradles the ghost of a sea.
Shoosh. Stop your girning!

A sharp night
That blade of new moon
shaving the star-stubbled cheek
of a wintry sky.

Swan's Way
See how the first line
of the canal's long poem
starts: a fancy S.

Still waters
the heart of the loch
is stunned that we have just glimpsed
its most secret joy.

James McGonigal
i.m. R. Gomez de la Serna

The power lines stretched
across the kingdom of frost
north of all music.

The sun is low now.
Our shadows are giants.
Soon all will be shadow.

Oak trees and the moon.
Light. Silent constellations.
And the cold ocean.

Working up the slopes
in open sunlight – the goats
that foraged on fire.

Tomas Tranströmer
translated by Robin Fulton

Haiku Envoi

The sea trembles – voiceless
It is the rare moment
when a word is sought

Concrete Haiku

Summer Haiku

P o o l .
P e o p l
  e   p l o p !
C o o l .

Edwin Morgan

Muezzin-cry

Swaying
   Pure
        Endless

Suhayl Saadi

January
snow
flake
drops

Gael Turnbull

After Basho
wind
blown
cloud

Davy Polmadie

from Spring Verses

April
already
nettles

*

tumbledown
shooting-butt
hut

*

pine
needle
path

*

daffo-
dils on
all day

wood pigeon
clapped
its wings

*

thin
autumn
wind

*

under
arrest
by ice

*

foot
following
foot

Three Line Poems

The Gazehound
the silver hound died in my arms
I breathed in her last breath
she looks out through my eyes

Valerie Gillies

Common Knowledge
The language of flowers is hermetic of insects vernacular
of fishes classic of grasses didactic of birds
oracular.

Edward Nairn

Prozac
So bright and buoyant –
hard orange plastic buoy
bobbing on a flat calm sea.

Andrew Greig

Waves
A slocken smile, scaled frae a burnie's mou
Waves rowe the crib o simmer
Saft as oo.

Sheena Blackhall

Confused by the rhythm
of other poets
I come to the stream.

Jayne Wilding

A Leid Ca'd Love
It's no your creed
and it's never your airt,
mak your leid cam fae your hert.

William Hershaw

Islandman

I am an uninhabitit island,
nae human markins oan my tidal sand.
Migrant geese sail abuin my barren land.

Robert Davidson

aig ceann taigh Tharscabhaig

tha Canaigh a' laighe beusach sa chuan
a' deàlradh mar nighean rudeigin tapaidh chèin
ach an tìr as fhaisge 's e do làmhan treun ann an grèin na maidne

Tarskavaig house end

Canna is lying modest in the sea
shining like a somewhat self-sufficient distant young woman
but the closest land your daring hands in the morning sun

John S. MacPherson

Five Crags
The five black angels of Hoy
That fishermen avoid –
The Sneuk, The Too, The Kame, Rora, The Berry.

Crofter-Fisherman
Sea-plough, fish-plough, provider
Make orderly furrows.
The herring will jostle like August corn.

New Boat
We call this boat Pigeon.
Go gentle, dove
Among skuas, easterlies, reefs, whalebacks.

Fishmonger
The fishmonger stood at the rock
With bits of dull silver
To trade for torrents of uncaught silver.

George Mackay Brown

Epigrams & Epitaphs

Mottoes: after Martial

Dumb-bells (XIV. xlix)
Leave the dumb dumb-bells to the chaps at the gym –
trenching vineyards will keep you in better trim.

Mushrooms (XIII. xlviii)
There's no problem sending clothes and money:
mushrooms go Parcel Force cepes delivery.

Torch (XIV. lxi)
So take this torch to light your way at night:
it's shockproof, like my heart, and weathertight.

Dormouse (XIII. lix)
I'm fast asleep in winter, when it seems
all I need to fatten me up is dreams.

Martial (c. 40-104 AD)
translated by Hamish Whyte

Pamphilus
Some, Ladies wed, some love, and some adore them,
I like their wanton Sport, then care not for them.

William Drummond (1585-1649)

Epitaph Extempore, on a person nicknamed the Marquis
Here lies a mock Marquis whose titles were shamm'd,
If ever he rise it will be to be damn'd.

Epitaph
Lo worms enjoy the seat of bliss
Where lords and lairds afore did kiss.

Robert Burns (1759-1796)

On Having Piles
Ah dextrous Chirurgeons, mitigate your plan:
Slice bullocks' rumps – but spare the rump of man.

Sir Walter Scott (1770-1832)

The Shoreless Sea
Above the darkness and earth's wandering hull
A frail moon hovers like a lonely gull.

Life
There is a darkness in the glittering air:
The feathers fall, the song is everywhere.

The Pool
Not only depth but stillness must be there
If the mind's pool would show life's image clear.

The Foundation
All structures of the mind, however vast,
Have sure foundation only in the breast.

Courage
Man's courage gleams, from greater misery,
As a white gull against a darkening sky.

William Soutar (1898-1943)

I

We're a'e clan here: I micht as weel
Ha'e been a Campbell as a McNeill.

II

Alas that life is past
Noo I'm a laird at last.

III

I'm deid, no daft, and dinna need
A folly o' flooers aboot my heid.

IV

Here lie MacDonalds glad to tine
A' that's become o' Scotland syne.

V

Croon me wi' blackthorn noo; in life
Droighneach resisted a' my strife.

VI

Nae man that wants to ha'e ideas
Aboot life efter daith sud wait till he dees.

Hugh MacDiarmid (1892-1978)

from Scotched

Scotch God
Kent His
Faither.

Scotch Star-Trek
Kent his
Phaser

Scotch Education
I tellt ye
I tellt ye.

Scotch Passion
Forgot
Mysel.

Scotch Gaeldom
Up the
Erse.

Scotch Astrology
Omen
In the gloamin.

Alexander Scott

Sunday Ferries
Every which way
but Lewis.

Angus Macmillan

Turner Prize
A coo and a cauf
Cut in hauf.

William Hershaw

Insert the Name of Your Favourite Scottish Poet
Las hing we need's anither _____ ,
An anither, an anither, an anither.

Robert Crawford

Villon and After
When it all comes out like cattle pish or addled
water: plenty of it – none worth drinking.

Alexander Hutchison

The Film-Maker Jan Švankmajer
he's the ivy tree of allegory
he's the lemon peel of the surreal

Valerie Gillies

The Love Song of Daniel O'Bese
First my gone gaunt love made my weight
an ultimatum; and then a *casus belli.*

Donny O'Rourke

1.
"Mr Sulu, set the controls
To Economy Wash. We're about to venture
Where no man has gone before."

2.
Kirk to Enterprise: "I'm going back to my cabin
With a box of Kleenex. I want to experience
The loneliness of command."

3.
All crewmen report to the foredeck
For Mr Spock's lecture on masculinity,
'Getting in Touch with Emotion'.

Robert Crawford

Proverbs

Sean-Fhacail Ghàidhlig

Trì nithean brèagha: long fo sheòl,
craobh fo bhlàth, is duine
naomh air leabaidh-bàis.

Na trì nithean as suaraich' à th'ann:
uaisle gun chuid, marag gun gheir,
agus pòg o bhus lom.

'S fheàrr a bhith air iomall
a' phailteis na
an teis meadhain a' ghoirt

Anail a Ghàidheil –
air a' mhullach

The three most beautiful things:
a ship under sail,
a tree in blossom,
and a man of faith on his death-bed.

The three ugliest things:
pride without grounds,
a black pudding without fat,
and a kiss from a miserly mouth.

Better plenty's periphery
than the heart of poverty.

The Gael's breathing place –
on the very summit.

translated by kevin macneil

Proverbs, after Machado

Always today, always

*

Now Spring has arrived,
don't chew on the wax –
get out of the hive

*

After the life and the dream
comes what matters most:
the awakening

*

Hey – let's divide the work, so
the bad guys dip the arrows,
the good guys flex the bow . . .

*

Not the sunrise
but the waking bell

*

Take an old man's word:
not his advice

Trust twine sooner
than string.

*

Temper harshness with tolerance,
tolerance with justice.

*

If you want to avoid
the worst of the mud
walk in the ruts.

*

The wind is invisible
but we can see which way
the trees lean.

*

Be sure your Victories
will find you out.

Ian Hamilton Finlay

Proverbs

Time and Emotion study;
takes all day
and gets you nowhere.

Tessa Ransford

History Lesson
for Ken McLeod

And you'll have noticed, Ken,
the way is always smoother on the far side of the glen

Andrew Greig

Boxes
As origami boxes
between invisible hands
time crumples men.

Walter Perrie

Desire becomes sorrow
just as night follows day
and today becomes tomorrow.

Robin Robertson

Heaven is a wet
pavement with streetlights painting
people like ikons.

Hell is a cocktail
party where the hostess sweeps
new soul mates apart.

Purgatory is
standing standing standing in
a blind date doorway.

Death is I don't want
to see you any more so
vanish I mean it.

Life is the return
of a castaway against
all odds remembered.

Birth is a swishing
broom that leaves the womb a dark
silent waiting-room.

Edwin Morgan

Myth

I
I aften heard my mither wish we had a bath.

"We could keep the coal in it," she'd say.

II
My mither wis a great yin for day dreamin.

"If anely we had some coal," she'd say
"we could hae a fire."

Pishamoolog

Why is the dandelion called 'wet the bed'
And not something dignified instead?

Ramscooter

When you're ramscootered, you're on your knees
Completely vanquished by your enemies

Shriek Cock

By its skraik shall ye know it. No there's rarely any hush
The mating season's raucous for the Ulster mistle thrush

Tummock

A proper tummock, you can scarcely see at all
The bump in a bog, a marshy mound, a knubbly knoll

Donny O'Rourke

Glasgow Zen

On the oneness of self and universe

> IT'S AW WAN
> TAE ME

On the ultimate identity of
matter and spirit, form and void

> WHIT'S THE MATTER
> NUTHIN!

On the suchness of things

> AYE, THIS IS IT
> THIS IS THE THING

On identity and difference

> SIX AN
> HAUF A DOZEN

On the implicit dualism
of value judgements

> IT'S AWFUL
> GOOD

What can haill but canna hear?
And answer back but canna speer?

Answer: An echo

William Soutar (1898-1943)

Spaces

Spaces
What might be said and then awaiting

what has been said.

Such Days
Such days

a cat sniffs at.

From the Sanscrit
They find me crying and commiserate

but would I waste tears on less than joy?

Gael Turnbull

from the other side of The County, her sigh
the seagull's feather

which burnt a plane's engines

kevin macneil

overheard in a graveyard in harris
    this end o the road then

it is fae some

Sean Burn

The young woman looks left, then right

before picking her neighbour's flowers

Larry Butler

By High Ponds
Wisdom is the sweetie-wrapper

not the sweetie

Andrew Greig

First Meeting (Chaplinesque)
The hole in her sock

was his lovers' moon

Ian Hamilton Finlay

A Highland Metaphysician Goes Shopping
"Do you sell boots?"   "We do."

"I'll have two"

Ian McDonough

Wallace Stevens Defines the Exceptional Nature of the Scottish Poem
Not so much a peacock,

More of a grouse.

Alistair Fowler

Songs of Praise
Even in a Protestant church

– how many Madonnas!

Ian Hamilton Finlay

A Last Poem
The merely unspoken

now beyond utterance.

Gael Turnbull

Two Line Poems

Late Night Shipping Forecast
billows
pillows

Bridget Penney

The singing grass and the aching sky
Are waves that break upon the eye.

Katrina Porteous

A Valentine
Her handwriting: spring water.
(Her words, river-washed pebbles.)

Ian Hamilton Finlay

The tides I missed –
the slanting rain.

Kathleen Jamie

For December
The broken song is off its crutches.
The wood is lit and the fire catches.

Richard Price

a green beacon
stars   so close

Paul Rubie

The thunder breaks
The children scatter like ninepins

Elizabeth Burns

In deference to the godhead
the snow on the very mountain-top untouched.

Peter McCarey

Field Work
lapwing high
jonquil sky

Alan Riach

Alice's Nocturne
Do you think the moon
's going to come home with us?

Ken Cockburn

from A Semblance of Steerage

For the Rudder of a River-Boat
to imprint
remembered way

Rudder for a Mirror
a semblance of steering
provides procedure

Rudder in Mahogany
swung to pivot
on zinc splashed pintles

Early Side-Wheeler
Her pennants wave, her brasses gleam,
Her mill-wheel starts to turn the stream.

Trading Schooner
This vessel roots with two gold tusks.
(Below, the crew fight rats for husks.)

After W. S.
Golden lads and girls all must,
As balsa gliders, come to dust.

Ian Hamilton Finlay

Gun leasachadh

"a' chàr, faodaidh tu tilleadh aig àm sam bith."
"Gun chàr a bhith agam, cha robh mi riamh air falbh."

Cold Comfort

"With the car you can come home anytime."
"Without the car, I'd never have left."

Meg Bateman

Form

A new moon recovers the hare
from its absence in grass and water.

John Burnside

The Parents

I

My Rabia does all her homework after tea.
She'll go far.

II

My Mohammed doesn't bother
He knows it's his life.

Hamid Shami

Inge-Land

I

The Yud came from the Mim
And the Mim was winter.

II

Fae the mud ae Faisalabad
Will I mould the bones ae Glasgee

Suhayl Saadı

Mim is one of three primal letters in the Hebrew alphabet
symbolising winter. *Yud* is the first letter in the Tetragrammation
(YMVH) which is one of the names of God. *Inge* means raven.

Basho in Scotland
waiting for the peony
to drip

Kristeva in Scotland
waiting for the peenie
to drop

Young Politician
What a lovely, lovely moon.
And it's in the constituency too.

Alan Jackson

Cold Isn't It
wirraw init thigithir missyz
geezyir kross

Tom Leonard

B6318
soft verges
severe dips

blind summits
lowland slopes

inky purple shadows
golden ash trunks

David Bellingham

the grey of distance
the taste of brambles

birch saplings rising
rain steadily falling

the miles at my back
the rain in my face

coming down to the water's edge
remembering an old tune

little dance in light
little song in shade

the moss on the gravestone
the waters rushing by

Thomas A. Clark

from The Flora and Fauna of an Independent Scotland

Scots Pine
Aye. D'they no' jeest.

Wild Strawberry
A pickle
o' wee wersh yins.

Nettle
That'll larn ye
tae keep yir hauns aff.

Woodworm Beetle
Eaves puddin'
. . . rafters fur afters!

Dwarf Thistle
An' you can keep oot o' it
furra stert.

Creeping Thistle
Jist haud oan a wee minute
– Ah'm the Flooer o' Scotland

Black-Throated Diver
Waly. Waly. Waly.

Shag
Awa an' fuck yersel'.

Wheatear
Yir bum's oot the windae.

Mole
Goany gie's a light, Jim?

Domestic Cat
Buggeryjar . . . ya beauty!

Hedgehog
Yin fur the road, eh?

Psylocybin
Ah'll gie ye independence, mun.
Jist a wee puckle.

Douglas Lipton

One Line Poems & Monostichs

A Classic Monostich
Schooner, sail your snows to the Pole.

An Eighteenth Century Line on a Lukewarm Hotwaterbottle
The frigid sheet engulfs the feeble ray.

Apollo in Strathclyde
The wine-dark sea, the turnip-marbled field.

A One Line Poem for a Postie
On the uneven road the bobbing red sail of the postvan

Ian Hamilton Finlay

The day was midge still.

Jayne Wilding

Breathing is all, in the space it can fill.

Tracy Mackenna

Night steals about among the grasses.

J. B. Pick

The underwater clerestories of demolished church light.

Frank Kuppner

In the Garden at Chartwell
perforated petals of rain beaten blue poppies

David Bellingham

Chartwell: the former home of Winston Churchill

Selected Grasses

the fragrant glumes of sweet vernal grass

*

the silver leaves of blue fescue

*

the nodding spikes of wild oat

*

the sharp awns of meadow barley

*

the sheathed stems of marram grass

*

the soft panicles of yorkshire fog

*

the waving plumes of common reed

*

the swollen fruits of yellow sedge

Thomas A. Clark

The acorn does not ask the oak for permission to grow.

*

In September here the river meadows are punctuated by sheep, piebald cattle and crows.

*

The cadence of rain at night on the metal roof has the flow of voices at a party.

*

Mist settles on the glen and all discourse ceases.

*

What I cannot possess alive I need only outlive.

*

Events have finally overtaken the oak and the thistle.

One-Word Poems

Two Evergreen Horizons

Neat Norwegian Horizon
spruce

Sad Scotch Horizon
pine

An Infinite Territory Between Two Ideals
grey

David Bellingham

A Grey Shore Between Day and Night
dusk

Ian Hamilton Finlay

October Evening, Shifting Leaves
susurrus

Robert Davidson

The Stones of the Field are the Birds of the Air
peewits

Ian Hamilton Finlay

Where It Rains
here

Where The Rainbow Ends
there

Gael Turnbull

Happy One-Word Poem
periwinkle

Dilys Rose

Down to Earth but Close to Heaven
bog-cotton

Davy Polmadie

April
apparition

Valerie Gillies

A Latent Snow Drift
alyssum

David Bellingham

The Burns are Low, Although the Banks Swell
meadowsweet

Alistair Peebles

Two Owls in a Fir Tree Smiling, Smiling
noughts

Giles Gordon

The Cloud's Anchor
swallow

Curfew
curlew

Deep-Vee Hull
geese

The Boat's Blueprint
water

A Patch for a Rip-tide
sail

Channel Light-Vessel Automatic
romance

Shaped by Locality
workboat

Shaped by Technology
yacht

Three Epitaphs

A Poem of Praise for George Mackay Brown
mass

A Poem of Recognition for Sorley Maclean
craobh

A Poem of Remembrance for Christopher Murray Grieve
headstone

The Man with Seagulls
ploughman

The Man with Rooks
sower

The Crucified Gentleman
scarecrow

Fish Floor
carpet

Fish Bird
swordfinch

The Dear Green Plaice
glasgow

Dangerous Glory
morning

A Far Cool Beautiful Thing, Vanishing
blue

What I Need to Cover This Decently
scrim

Alexander Hutchison

Condition of Lester Young before and after Billie Holiday taunted
Coleman Hawkins into a sax battle with him in the late-night jazzers' bar.
cut

Angus Calder

The Prime Minesterial Apple of Discord
luvviedome

Drew Milne

In the Strathtyrum Museum of Gender
bluestocking

Robert Crawford

The Satellite
medusa

Kevin Henderson

Pull the Other One
tug

Colin Dunning

North Sea Potato
Rigsmash

Hamish Whyte

Field Garment
wind-sock

Davy Polmadie

Seed
y

Sex
y

A Sampler of Simple Stitches
summer

A Lover of Shade
honesty

A Night-Scented Water Lily
moon

An Aromatic Seasoning
thyme

Dicotyledons

mist
mint

spectrum
plectrum

wanting
waiting

jonquil
tranquil

Thomas A. Clark

On Going to Meet a Zen Master in the Kyushu
Mountains and Not Finding Him

for A. G.

Appendices

About Nothing In Particular

to make a short song
out of nothing, a few words
to keep me going
to take nothing's notation
is a mile's occupation

the thistle and gorse
the kiss, the blessing, the curse
are built on nothing
the cairn, the old fort, the hill
the tibia of the gull

that water is best
that bubbles up out of rock
tasting of nothing
in a lull in a cold wind
I have stretched out to drink it

        convolvuulus stems
the complexities of thought
        old country dances
weave figures around nothing
bring plenitude from nothing

        you are my good friend
the best of company on
        the long shore road home
when there is nothing to say
you stay quiet and easy

        just before the dawn
I woke to the sound of rain
        and knowing nothing
of my location or shape
like the grass I was refreshed

Three Cinquains

Miracle
Summer
Is on the hill;
But in the moveless air
The fountain of the hawthorn hangs
With frost.

Beyond Legend
What surge
Is in our blood:
And in our flesh what loam;
Tides from Atlantis and the dust
Of Ur.

The Mask
They look
With tenderness
On time's deformities
Who see love's face behind the mask
Of clay.

William Soutar

Commentaries

'haiku are weeds along life's highway'

Basho

'A real haiku's gotta be as simple as porridge and yet make you see the real thing, like the greatest haiku of them all probably is the one that goes: "The sparrow hops along the veranda, with wet feet." *By Shiki. You see the wet footprints like a vision in your mind and yet in those few words you also see all the rain that's been falling that day and almost smell the wet pine needles.'*

Jack Kerouac, The Dharma Bums

Haiku

'Haiku is a finger pointing at the moon, but if the hand is bejewelled we no longer see that to which it points.'

R. H. Blyth

Some years ago I came near to poetic despair. It seemed to me that the main trends in so-called post-modern poetry were leading away, wilfully, from the pure and eternal wells of Poesy into a profitless desert. Formlessness, meaninglessness, obscurantism, vulgarity of language and, particularly, an all too frequent atmosphere of mawkish self-pity, all repelled me. I could not follow. Yet I still wanted to write.

Somehow, it seemed a small miracle at the time, I discovered classical haiku. These superficially simple, austere little tercets by the old Japanese masters, Basho, Buson, Issa and Shiki, were curiously potent. As I allowed them to flower in my mind unexpected layers of connection and meaning revealed themselves. With the thrill I found myself at one with the spirit of those great but humble practitioners.

Then it became clear that the ancient haiku tradition had never died, had indeed gone through several subsequent thoroughgoing reassesments and was more alive than ever, not only in Japan but all over the world. Hoping to make a contribution of my own one day, I began to study the form.

I quickly realised that in the West misconceptions were common. Perhaps more importantly, dictionaries lay down that a haiku must contain seventeen syllables in a rigid three-line pattern of 5-7-5. But this is based on the idea that a Japanese 'syllable' can be equated with a linguistic unit so described in other languages. One has only to understand, for example, that our monosyllabic word 'rain' can contain up to three syllables by Japanese reckoning 'R-AI-N' to see the falsity of the 5-7-5 stricture. In fact, well realised haiku in English often work out at 10 to 14 syllables, as we evaluate them phonetically. Padding with unnecessary words is the antithesis of the haikuist's minimalist art.

I soon noticed divergent tendencies in regard to subject matter. Some Western poets who had adopted the haiku vehicle, particularly in the USA, were mistakenly dealing in sexual fantasy, solipsism, anthropomorphism, aphoristic squibs, vague abstractions. All these are quite foreign to haiku, which concerns itself with concrete images, textures, smells, sounds, tastes. It is also unfailingly well-mannered. Tercets lacking a nature reference and often revealing personal attitudes are termed senryu and regarded quite separately in Japan.

One famous haiku by Matsuo Basho (1644-94) conveys more about this mode of poetic expression than a volume of instruction:

This quietness:
the shrilling of cicadas
stabs into the rocks

First, the poem is set squarely in the world of Nature. As urban civilisation has developed and the centuries have passed, this mandatory requirement has been somewhat diluted, but it is remarkable how often a nature reference, or at least a seasonal one, still surfaces in the work of even the most innovative haikuists of today. This involvement with Nature is not of a detached, Wordsworthian character but is an intimate and intense self-identification with the objects observed, animate or inanimate. The poet seeks to see deep into the bird's being, or that of the flower, the lake, the rock. He does not try to explain, except maybe by subtle implication, any effect which his feelings of kinship with these objects may be having on him. If the moment is captured, that is enough.

In other words, haiku typically externalises, more or less suppresses Self, in contradistinction to the defining characteristic of much contemp-orary Western verse, performance poetry and the like.

The early influences on haiku were many: Confucianism, Taoism, Chinese/Japanese Zen Buddhism, other strands of traditional Eastern wisdom, lighthearted teahouse entertainments, calligraphy, painting. As a result it is not surprising that attitudes among Western poets vary widely, from, at one extreme, a dedicated Buddhistic view that haiku is far closer to religion than poetry, to the severely secularist opinion which holds that it is simply one type of literary expression.

My own position is somewhere in the middle of that spectrum. Undoubtedly the best haiku, contemporary as well as ancient, can provoke insights, sublime revelations about man's place in the scheme of things, which border on the numinous. Equally, however, many fine poems set out to do no more than delight through their acute descriptions and contrasts, their artful, sometimes enigmatic concision. It seems to me that both varieties of epiphany are utterly valuable to the reader or listener in this hectic, noisome world.

Moods which most frequently occur in true haiku are compassion, serenity, humility, paradox, wonder, acceptance, joy and occasionally, a gentle humour.

This is a haiku written in America (by Bruce Ross) not so long ago, which I believe can stand comparison with the classical models:

Autumn drizzle:
the slow ticking
of the clock

Can't you see the cold rain filtering down hour after hour? The poet's presence in his room is only hinted at. Perhaps the remorseless tick-tock of the clock comforts him/her, or is it getting on his/her nerves? What is he/she thinking about? The haikuist leaves all that to the reader's imagination. And no doubt similar situations will be awakened in the reader's consciousness.

As I progressed a little in the composition of haiku in English a Scots word often occurred to me as the better expressing more exactly or more succinctly what I wished to convey. Like all Scots brought up in their own country I found I possessed a reservoir of Scots vocabulary at the back of my mind. So I tried tentatively to write haiku in Scots. This in turn led me to confer on my poems, here and there, a few 'Scotch' idiosyncrasies, like an awareness of Scotland's beauty but also of the unending struggle in Nature, a certain preoccupation with the ghoulish and a wry familiarity with death. The Auld Leid and the ancient haiku form seemed to fuse felicitously:

Loch o jeel
braw wi gowden sin:
i the wuids hairts dee

Bruce Leeming

Haiku

The first time I ever came across haiku I was still at school. I was 17, my head full of Dylan Thomas's 'ferocious, ununderstandable' verse. A school friend who was an artist showed me a graphics magazine he was reading and in it was a full-page advertisement for Day-Glo paper. (This was 1965!) As I remember it, the top half of the page was a virulent orange, the bottom half was an equally virulent lime green, and they flickered and clashed against each other in good psychedelic style. Across the top half were three small dark specks, and across the bottom half, a three line poem about crows against the evening sky. It wasn't poetry as I un-understood it, but something in that simple stark image stayed with me, a piece of poetic grit at the edge of my consciousness.

In 1967, by which time I was at University, I was reading books on Zen – Paul Reps, *Zen Flesh Zen Bones*, Alan Watts, *The Way of Zen* – blue-covered Pelican paperbacks I still own. The Watts book had a chapter specifically on haiku, and I was making the connection between haiku and a state of mind, a state of being – clear-eyed seeing into 'the life of things.'

In 1968, another friend loaned me a book of haiku translations by R. H. Blyth, a beautiful edition published in Japan by Hokuseido. The books were expensive (£2.50, at a time when paperbacks were 15p!). But I managed to put money aside, and over several trips to London (hitch-hiking) I made the pilgrimage to Compendium in Camden Town, bought all four (one at a time) and carted them back to Glasgow in my rucksack. It was money, and time, well spent. Along with his own quirky translations – lucid, pared down renditions into English – Blyth included the original Japanese in kanji script and phonetically transcribed romaji, so you got the look, and by reading them out loud, the sound, of the original. He also linked the poems with his own dazzlingly erudite gloss, but these never detracted from the poems themselves.

Also in 1968, I wrote some haiku of my own. The first came about almost by accident. I'd written a little two verse poem about autumn. The first verse was forgettable. (I've forgotten it!) It can't have been any good. But the second verse was as follows:

Damp leaves drift
to earth / the
sun hangs tangled
in the branches
of a tree

Something made me count the syllables. 17. A pure, unconscious haiku. I wrote a few more, all sticking strictly to the 17-syllable count, though not to the three line, 5-7-5 structure. (I'd also been reading Carlos Williams and Creeley, and was conscious of the look of the thing on the page. The spacing was often a function of the rhythm, the way I thought it should sound – spaces and pauses indicated by line endings but also by oblique / slashes).

Initially I stuck rigorously to the 17-syllable count. But there would be times when I'd be ruining a perfectly good poem by ripping out a word (or forcing one in). So I started approximating the count – 15 or 18, what did it matter as long as long as the rhythm was right? Then on re-reading the Blyth translations, I decided syllable counting was beside the point. I think there's such a thing as a haiku rhythm – you can hear when it's right, and division into lines on the page reflects that.

The eye and ear are equally important. What I've evolved towards is a three line form, usually, not more than 17 syllables long (or short). The important thing is the content, catching those little existential moments of insight, what Basho called the ah! of things.

The first haiku I wrote (that autumn one quoted above, later rearranged into 3 lines) appeared with my second, a winter haiku, in the 1969 volume of the annual Scottish Poetry anthologies published by EUP. (Lovely wee hardbacks, these appeared over 8 or 9 years then stopped).

Over the 30 years since I started writing them, I've continued to produce haiku alongside my novels, short stories and plays. In some ways they're the heart of my writing. They've appeared in a number of small magazines (anthologies tend to pass over short poems generally) and in three small-press collections of my own – plop! (a little pamphlet published by Tom And Maureen McGrath's Midnight Press in 1970), *ah!* (a paperback of 50 haiku printed by Sri Chimnoy's Agni Press in New York in 1975) and *Glasgow Zen* (Glasgow Print Studio Press, 1981). All of these are long out of print, but I often do haiku at readings, in amongst the longer stuff, and they work really well, dropped into the silence. There's an audience for haiku out there.

Alan Spence

Haiku

After some years of trying to write haiku, I gave up, and found myself writing haiku! The 17 syllable package didn't seem to work for me, until I forgot about it. Then, when a few scattered poems fell into this pattern, it was possible to add more, to extend them into a series, with relative facility. This is often how a form occurs.

My poems in this form are perceptions not, as is usually the case with Western haiku, gems of wisdom. It is unclear whether the content, wrenched from its ground, is at all exemplary, but this is the only way that I can write – forward, into the adventure of writing. In other words, a poem should not be over before it is begun.

The great writers of haiku were famous for sitting or walking, two activities which emphasise the solitary human figure. Walking or sitting, they held themselves apart from every complacency. That separate perceptions amount to a world, that there is an object for longing, they did not assume but tested, again and again, each one, alone.

Thomas A. Clark

Haiku

Despite what some people have said about me, I've never thought that haiku is the only form of poetry possible today, and, far from being an absolute adept of minimalism, I'm not only interested in the long poem, I actually practise it. No, it's because outside haiku's intrinsic essence (which is not too easy to get at), haiku practice, even imperfectly performed, saves us from a kind of 'poetry' that is so much lumber in the mind. When people send me their manuscripts of poetry, I often suggest they drop their lamentations, their elucubrations, their verbal accumulations, and get out on the haiku path. The result may not always be great right away, but the disencumberment in itself is welcome, and a benefit. What is more, haiku can usefully be practised by intelligent and sensitive people who would fight shy of the word 'poetry', but who feel the need to note some moment that marked their minds and allowed them to rise up out of the sentimental confusion, the ideological fog and the tangled identity complexes we usually call 'life', and out of which we often make 'literature'. Haiku means a little light, a gust of fresh air, a sense of openness.

Kenneth White

from Some Reflections on the Distinctive Features of British Haiku

The British have a knack for senryu; 'haiku' remains the best label we have, [and] it is right to include even obvious senryu under the umbrella . . . There is something about haiku, pure haiku as opposed to senryu, which keeps company with monks, beggars and hermits, and shuns the limelight. Senryu is pointed; haiku is pointless; senryu is hard, haiku is soft; senryu is punchy, haiku is weightless; you can get a kick out of senryu, but haiku is intangible and evanescent; senryu can make you laugh, haiku struggles to raise a half-smile.

Martin Lucas

Haiku and Epigrams

If you were looking for 'ancestors' so to speak, then the Gaelic and Scots proverbs (admittedly in an oral and entirely 'non-modernist' tradition) are as rich as you'll find. Gaelic and Irish culture have a liking for triadic forms and sayings, which are a bit more imagination-expanding and formal than the handed-down quality of the proverbial tradition. Epigrams are much more considered, 'literary' and self-conscious things . . . Kenneth Jackson's *A Celtic Miscellany* has a section on Celtic epigrams and most of these would seem to be two and four line. Traditional epigrams work best when at their most succinct, self-complete and forceful. In this respect I think that they probably belong in the same category as aphorisms (and perhaps epitaphs, mock epitaphs and proverbs). These forms – and especially epigrams – depend on a witty closure, most often signalled by a closing rhyme, or a couplet – e.g. Ogden Nash's: *'Senescence begins / And middle age ends / The day your descendants / Outnumber your friends.'*

Compared to this epigrammatic impulse, the one line, two line, and haiku type poem works in a completely opposite way – an opening up, a sense of space and indeed 'unclosure' which is a crucially different effect, with an even more crucially different ontological position behind it.

Roderick Watson, extracts from a letter to the editor.

Neil Gunn

In *Highland River*, Gunn uses Hindu Yoga (the 'religion' not the exercises), not Zen, as a point of comparison for Kenn's walk up the hillside to the source of his childhood river. "I have observed the way some of your Celtic poets have lately been inclined towards the East. You had better be careful" says Radzyn, Kenn's main interlocutor in the book. Note the authorial distance of that . . . the outsider, Radzyn, might well make the simplistic connection between the 'Celt' and the 'East', but Kenn, and I think Gunn, is more ironic, though not wholly negative either . . . Gunn didn't engage with Zen as such until much later – 1953 . . . when J. B. Pick sent him Herrigel's *Zen and the Art of Archery* . . . He only had one novel left to write, as well as the extraordinary *Atom of Delight* (I am still not sure whether one shouldn't count that as an experiment in fiction, too!) . . . If Zen does have affinities with 'Scottish experience' it also has great affinities with the modernist epiphany, and its precursor, Imagism . . . economy of means: 'the ultimate inspired simplicity, economy, of the single brush stroke.' For some reason I think of W. C. Williams here, and of Williams's enthusiasm for Gunn's *The Drinking Well* (though I wouldn't have chosen that baggy monster as the best example of Gunn's concision!) . . .

Richard Price, extracts from a letter to the editor.

Bodhidharma came from the west

Bodhidharma came from the west, and although the transmission of the dharma is reckoned in lineages, these lines cross, recross, become a multidimensional web – Indra's net – with someone at every join.

How the dharma came to Scotland (in one form, Zen Buddhism, and thus haiku) could be reckoned by tracing back along one strand of the web, but would by ignoring other strands and influences, be more or less arbitrary.

Bodhidharma came from the west, and that lineage is still moving eastward, from India, through Asia (the 'far east') Japan, W. Coast America, where the first Asian immigrants founded a temple in San Francisco in 1853. By the turn of the century, Buddhist teachers began to arrive there – Nyogen Senzaki and Daisetz Suzuki among them. Picking strands becomes difficult here. Suzuki's writings (from 1907 to 1973) slowly began to reach a large audience; one of Senzaki's students was Albert Saijo, a friend of Jack Kerouac whose own idiosyncratic studies of Buddhism helped form American attitudes to Zen (and haiku). Of course American writers were already aware of the dharma – Thoreau, and Emerson had seen to that; Pound, in Europe through Fenollosa, and imagism made further connections.

The publication of *Zen in English Literature and Oriental Classics* by R. H. Blyth (English by birth) in 1942 is a big join in our net. His four-volume *Haiku* (1949-52) introduced a new generation to haiku (and then Zen; the reverse of what had previously happened). Oral transmissions have not happened in the west so much since Caxton; most of us get a little of what we want from the written word. The availability of Blyth's work to my generation, in these islands, having reached this far from the west by the late 1950s, was our first taste of haiku. The small books of the *Wisdom of the East* series from a London publishing house (John Murray) continued the work, with books like Lewis Mackenzie's *The Autumn Wind* (1957), translations of the poems of Issa, as did Henderson's *An Introduction to Haiku* in 1958. *The Penguin Book of Japanese Verse* in 1964 widened the net.

Like many others at the time, I was struck by Kerouac's *Dharma Bums*, with its romantic descriptions of how haiku could be written by westerners. This reached us here about the same time as another book, (where else could we go at that time for such ideas?) Lucien Stryk & Takashi Ikemoto's *Zen: Poems, Prayers, Sermons, Anecdotes, Interviews*, which did so much to present traditional models and poetic possibilities. Books opened thick and fast then. We went back to sources where we could, again through the written word, books like Suzuki's *Zen and Japanese Culture* and *The Zen Doctrine of No Mind*; like Shunryu Suzuki's *Zen Mind Beginner's Mind*. And through Kerouac we had discovered Snyder, Whalen, Ginsberg, Saijo and a host of others. We also began to sit, and to write – haiku among other things. We found a freedom within a rigorous and alien form which we made our own; adapted and experimented with. Sitting, writing & reading, I was increasingly aware of a small number of individuals working in similar spaces, Ian Hamilton Finlay, Alan Spence, Chris and Val Torrance, Bill Wyatt, Thomas A. Clark (to name only a few), experimenting with short forms and haiku – expressing something that was, for me at least, lacking in the so-called mainstream literature of the day, a way of life, a way of seeing.

Gerry Loose

Scottish Journey

Wind is to me something that ruffles up the collars of our shirts, that moves the waters as they need moving. Of those of us who do not live there, who is there who goes to Scotland for sedation? We go, do we not, like Basho went to Michinoku, to be tattered and torn and purged and washed, and perhaps even to be baptized. That summer-cum-winter when I went with Kaz, a tent and a car, a hole was blown in me, a hole through which light, smoke and rainwater can, now and forever, freely, inexorably seep.

Tito

Wee Poems

I was talking to Alan Spence last year about haikus, and he recalled . . . giving a reading with Norman MacCaig some years back, and as he read his poems he could clearly see Norman syllable-counting. In the interval Norman said, "Those aren't haikus, Alan. Those are wee poems."

Colin Will, extract from a letter to the editor.

Other Forms

Why 'Spaces'?

Because we apprehend the text visually, and although we may 'sound' the poem, must finally 'hear' it with our inward ear. The space is thus a gap, a pause, even a hesitation, perhaps something unsaid or implied. A temporary dislocation of attention? It may serve in different ways. In the more successful examples, something occurs between the first line and the last. A change of tack, a tension? The difficulty is to avoid having the structure drift into merely an epigram or imagist poem, even haiku, so that the space is mere inflation, attention seeking, of no more use than the ordinary visual device of dividing a text into lines.

Gael Turnbull

A Conversation in an Orchard

The one line poem or monostich, goes on bravely, for as long as it goes on. It does not hook over or link up with a following concept or perception to become part of any discourse. It is one unit of sense, more often a phrase than a sentence. Breaking out of silence, avoiding closure, like a far horizon, it covers enough ground to support a patch of sky.

While drawing attention to itself by its brevity, the monostich addresses something beyond language, and is frugal with the play of syllables and words. A delay, or gate, at different moments it may be shut or open, open or shut. Less to be read than looked at, it outlasts the gaze to linger in reflection.

Thomas A. Clark

from 'Sonnet is a Sewing-Machine for the Monostich': On Some Monostichs by Ian Hamilton Finlay

The monostich is a poem of one line, a poetical form rarely used but nevertheless of formal interest. An often quoted example is the alexandrine Apollinaire wrote in praise of the trumpet shell in *Alcools*, but this is in fact the only monostich one can find in Apollinaire's writing.

Far more pertinent is the reference to Emmanuel Lochac who conceived a great part of his work in the form of monostichs, the rest being . . . made up of short poetical forms, maxims, notes, sixaines, and so on. Born in Kiev in 1886, Lochac lived in France from 1894 and wrote (in French), intimate confiding compositions akin to those of that other enthusiast of short literary forms, Francois Dodat. The first of Lochac's monostichs probably illustrates the essentials of the form:

Many a poem is the cage in which a captive verse sings

Besides the beautiful metaphor equating the lines of the text with the bars of the cage, one will think here of Valery's well known theory of the 'given line' – that is, the inspired line – and the calculated lines added as an explanatory afterthought.

Finlay's use of short forms preceded his discovery of Lochac, and it was natural that he should one day ask me to send him everything I could find on that writer. What surprised me was that a request concerning a writer so little known in the French-speaking world should come from Scotland. I had already observed Finlay's interest in fragmentation: detached sentence, (imitation) dictionary definition, one-word poem, each of these solutions presents its own advantages.

As for the monostich, it relates directly to more conventional poetry, and one will find in it, for example, echoes of the couplet. For if there is only one line, there are nearly always two syntactic units linked together, so much so that the monostich often finishes up as a distich: 'water-cooled / watercress' or 'pastor of oaks / shepherd of stones'. This pairing is the very essence of rhetoric since the two sides of a multiple meaning have to be present: the literal and the figurative.

Francis Edeline, extract from a catalogue essay for an exhibition at the Crawford Arts Centre, St Andrews, 1993.

One-Word Poems

Dear Ernst – Among the POTHs [*Poor. Old. Tired. Horse.* – the poetry magazine Finlay published in the 1960s] to come you will see that there will be one of poems of only one word . . . If you would like to send some poems for it I would be very pleased . . . I have gathered a number of very good examples of the form, but I would wish . . . to have as many poems as possible (as a little change from the white spaces of concrete [poetry]) . . . The kind of poem I would most like is a serious one, for many people have sent examples which are only briefly witty, and the form is capable of more than that. After all one has the whole title to move around in . . . I got very fascinated by it, for it has haiku-brevity, without reading like a pseudo-Japanese poem. Or in another way, it is very close to the classical epitaph or epigram . . .

Ian Hamilton Finlay, extract from a letter to Ernst Jandl, 1966 (*Chapman magazine*, No. 78/79, 1994)

Index of Authors

Acknowledgements

Thanks are due to the following copyright holders for permission to reproduce the poems in this collection. While every effort has been made to trace and credit copyright holders, the Publishers will be glad to rectify any oversights in any future editions.

STEVE ALLAN: *A Thimble Full of Letters.* DAVID BELLINGHAM: (from various postcards and folding cards, WAX366, 1997-99). SHEENA BLACKHALL: p43 *Back o' Bennachie* (Hammerfield Publishing, 1993); p107 *The Life Bluid o' Cromar* (1997); GEORGE MACKAY BROWN: p109 *Fishermen With Ploughs* (© Hogarth Press, 1971). GEORGE BRUCE: *Pursuit* (© Scottish Cultural Press, 1999). JOHN BURNSIDE: *The Myth of the Twin* (© Jonathan Cape/Random House, 1994). MYLES CAMPBELL: *A' Caradh an Rathaid/Ag Coiru an Roid* (© COISCEUM, 1988). THOMAS A. CLARK: *Alder Roots* (Moschatel Press, 1998); *Selected Grasses* (MP, 1998); *Two Evergreen Horizons* (MP, 1979); p173 *A Still Life* (Jargon Society, 1977); *Dicotelydons* (MP, 1981); *About Nothing in Particular* (Morning Star Publications, 1990; © Polygon, 1993); *Conversation in an orchard* (MP, 1998). LINDSAY COOPER: *Jail Poems.* ROBERT CRAWFORD: p119 *Masculinity* (© Jonathan Cape/Random House, 1998); p118 *Sharawaggi*, with W. N. Herbert, (© Polygon, 1990). CHRISTINE DE LUCA: *Voes & Sounds* (© The Shetland Library, 1995). ANGUS DUNN: *Eddies* (1998). IAN HAMILTON FINLAY: *Silhouettes* (Wild Hawthorn Press, 1974); *The Old Stonypath Hoy* (WHP, Christmas 1991); *Twilight* (WHP); *Two One Line Poems for Posties* (WHP, 1998); *Proverbs for Jacobins* (WHP); *More Proverbs for Jacobins* (WHP, 1992); p165 *Grains of Salt* (Oriel Mostyn, 1996). ALISON FLETT: (Jonathan Cape/Random House, 1997). DUNCAN GLEN: *Buits & Wellies* (© Akros, 1976). WILLIAM HERSHAW: p107 *The Cowdenbeath Man* (© Scottish Cultural Press, 1997). ALAN JACKSON: *All Fall Down* (The Kevin Press, 1965); *Salutations: Collected Poems* (© Polygon, 1990). KATHLEEN JAMIE: p61 *Black Spiders* (© Salamander Press, 1982). JACK KEROUAC:

TURNBULL: p101 *For Whose Delight* (© Mariscat, 1995). KENNETH WHITE: *L'Anorak du goëland* (© L'Instant Perpetuel, 1986); *Les Rives du Silence* (© Mercure de Paris, 1997); *Travels in the Drifting Dawn* (© Mainstream Publishing, 1989); *On Scottish Ground* (© Polygon, 1998). HAMISH WHYTE: p112 *A Gathering for Gael Turnbull* (Vennel Press, 1998). COLIN WILL: p56 in *Things Not Seen* (Aberdeenshire Council, 1999).

The publishers wish to thank the following magazines and journals in which some of these poems originally appeared: *Blithe Spirit; Chapman Magazine; The Edinburgh Review; Glasgow University Magazine; Haiku Magazine; Haiku Quarterly; Haiku Spirit; Hummingbird; Modern Haiku; Object Permanence; Poor.Old.Tired.Horse; Roy Rogers; Sesheta; snapshots.*

pocketbooks

Summer 1998

01   GREEN WATERS
      An anthology of boats and voyages, edited by Alec Finlay;
      featuring poetry, prose and visual art by Ian Stephen,
      Ian Hamilton Finlay, Graham Rich.
      ISBN 0 9527669 2 2; paperback, 96pp, colour illustrations, reprinting.

Spring 2000

02   ATOMS OF DELIGHT
      An anthology of Scottish haiku and short poems, edited with an
      Introduction by Alec Finlay, and a Foreword by Kenneth White.
      ISBN 0 7486 6275 8; paperback, 208pp, £7.99.

03   LOVE FOR LOVE
      An anthology of love poems, edited by John Burnside and
      Alec Finlay, with an Introduction by John Burnside.
      ISBN 0 7486 6276 6; paperback, 200pp, £7.99.

04   WITHOUT DAY
      An anthology of proposals for a new Scottish Parliament, edited
      by Alec Finlay, with an introduction by David Hopkins. *Without
      Day* includes an Aeolus CD by William Furlong.
      ISBN 0 7486 6277 4; paperback with CD, 184pp, £7.99 (including VAT).

Autumn 2000

Available through all good bookshops.

Book trade orders to:
Scottish Book Source, 137 Dundee Street, Edinburgh EH11 1BG.

Copies are also available from:
Morning Star Publications, Canongate Venture (5), New Street,
Edinburgh EH8 8BH.

Website: www.pbks.co.uk

At the end,
There is only the book and the dust
And the wind